An Introduction to
Hardanger Embroidery

White Hardanger tablecloth – see page 28.

An Introduction to
HARDANGER EMBROIDERY

SEARCH PRESS

First published in Great Britain 1994

Search Press Limited
Wellwood, North Farm Road,
Tunbridge Wells, Kent, TN2 3DR

Reprinted 1997

English translation © Search Press Ltd. 1994

First published in Germany by Christophorus-Verlag
GmbH Freiburg im Breisgau, 1993, as *Das Hardanger-Buch
1: klassische Muster* (Edition Zweigart), Copyright ©
Christophorus-Verlag GmbH.

Embroidery designs by Bärbel Kreibich, Irmgard Gürtesch,
and Astrid Jannedy. Photographs by Thomas Schuster,
Sindelfingen, Germany.

The publishers would like to thank Artisan, 22 High Street,
Pinner, Middlesex HA5 5PJ, for their advice in the prepara-
tion of this book.

If you have difficulty in obtaining any of the materials
or equipment mentioned in this book, please write for
further information to the publishers.
Search Press Limited, Wellwood, North Farm Road,
Tunbridge Wells, Kent TN2 3DR, England.

ISBN 085532 782 0

Printed in Malaysia by Times Offset

Contents

Introduction

Hardanger embroidery is a form of openwork which originated in the Norwegian fiord country of Hardanger. It is a form of whitework and is traditionally embroidered using the white-on-white technique, on white or natural-coloured linen.

The women of Hardanger made latticed openwork with geometric motifs for their home and to decorate their regional costume, using only embroidery thread and linen that they had made themselves. The style involves interesting and unique combinations of flat openwork with dense, raised satin-stitch ornamentation and decorative cross-stitch motifs.

Some of the best-known traditional work is found in the exquisite aprons of the region, decorated with wide inset bands of Hardanger embroidery.

This attractive form of embroidery soon became popular outside Scandinavia as well around the turn of the century. At that time Hardanger work was mainly used to adorn cushions and tablecloths. Today its simple elegance has once again become extremely popular.

Hardanger embroidery can only be worked properly on a high-quality even-weave fabric which shows up the lace-like square openwork to its full advantage.

About Hardanger embroidery

In Hardanger work, first of all you secure the motifs by satin-stitch edging and only after that do you cut out the threads and make woven bars. Since you always come back to the point you started at when edging with satin stitch, you can check that you have not miscounted before you do any cutting out.

When using patterns with a lot of openwork, it is best to cut out only the parts that fit exactly in the embroidered frame, as the fabric loses stability because of the missing threads and is only properly strengthened again by binding. You really need to stick to the proper sequence of work.

You should use a blunt embroidery needle for this kind of work.

To make it easier for you to work from the pattern, the stitch-by-stitch charts are printed in square groups that simultaneously correspond to the satin-stitch groups typical of Hardanger embroidery.

Layout

Always start counting threads from the centre outwards. You should mark the centre lines given in each pattern with tacking.

Because the embroidery is based throughout on groups of four threads, when following the chart, use the formula '1 box = 4 threads'.

Buying material

When you are buying material, make sure that you take hem and seam allowances into account, and, depending on the size of what you are making, add 5–15cm (2–6in) of material, to be on the safe side.

Hardanger stitches ✛

Embroidery charts

The charts show a quarter or a half of the embroidery motif, as the case may be; the centre of the motif is marked in each case by a dotted red line. Other methods are also shown: for example, how to lay out the motifs to make other sizes of cloth.

Key

☐ 1 box = 4 threads of the fabric

▨ Cut out the threads of the fabric

▥ Satin-stitch groups = five stitches worked across four threads of the fabric

▱ Making a woven bar with four threads of the fabric

✥ Woven bars with dove's-eye filling stitch

Satin stitch

Satin-stitch motifs are worked in horizontal and vertical stitches, following the chart. You can get diagonals by shifting along satin stitches following one another diagonally by one thread.

Detailed drawings for satin stitch are shown thread by thread.

Satin-stitch border

Hardanger motif borders consist of groups of satin stitch worked five stitches over four threads of the fabric. They are worked alternately vertically and horizontally. Where the stitches adjoin at right angles, the first stitch of a group is worked into the same entry point as the last stitch of the previous group.

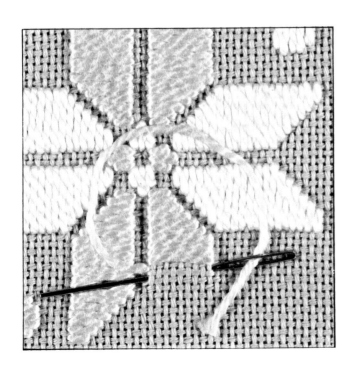

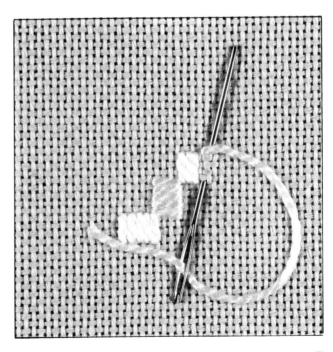

Cutting the threads

When you have secured all the edges with satin stitch, cut off the threads close to the groups of satin stitch with a pair of sharp-pointed scissors. Each time, cut groups of four threads. The groups of satin stitch running parallel to them secure the cut edges.

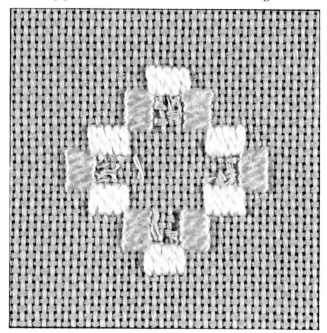

Pulling out the threads

Pull out the threads you have cut off inside the motif. This will give you a latticework of threads consisting of groups of four threads of the fabric.

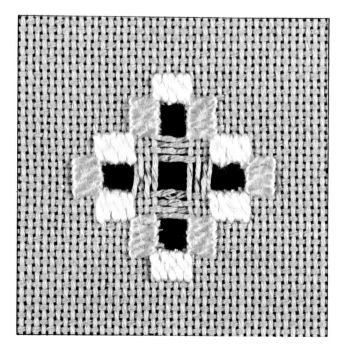

Woven bars

Secure the groups of four threads by weaving or binding. Take the needle down between two pairs of threads. Bring the needle up over one pair, down through the middle, and up over the other pair. Continue along the length of the bar, pulling the weaving tight to form a diagonal pattern.

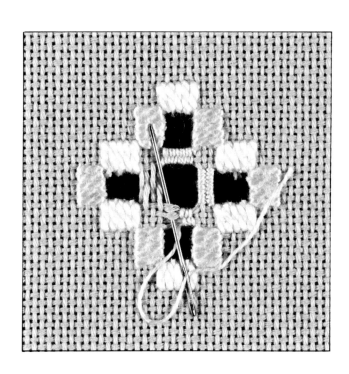

Woven bars with dove's-eye filling stitch

Bind the group of threads as described above but before you complete the last bar of a square, begin the dove's-eye filling stitch.

1. Bind the last bar to the middle, then form a loop in the centre of the design: pass the the needle down through the middle of the first bound bar and up over the embroidery thread. Pull the thread to form an arc. Now take the needle down through the middle of the second bound bar and up over the embroidery thread again to form another arc. Repeat at the third bound bar.

2. On the last bar, take the needle behind the first arc and down through the middle of the four remaining unbound threads. Finish the binding of the fourth bar as normal.

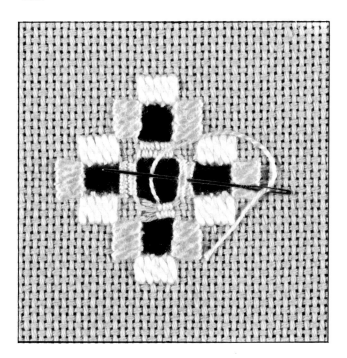

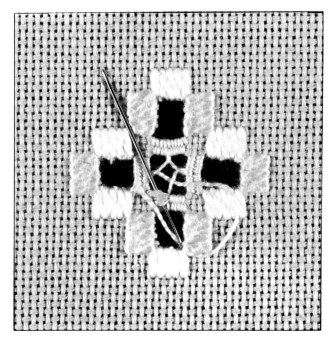

Buttonhole stitch

Zigzag borders (festoon borders, castellated borders) are worked in buttonhole stitch over four threads.

Bring your needle out at the required start point, pass it back down through the fabric, four threads up and one to the right, and bring it out again next to the point you started at. Complete the stitch by passing the needle over the loop in the embroidery thread and pulling the thread taut. Inside corners are worked twice through the same point of exit with the threads at right angles to each other. Outside corners have a common point of entry for five stitches, with the exit points shifting by two threads at a time. After you have finished the embroidery, cut the material away close to the buttonhole-stitch border.

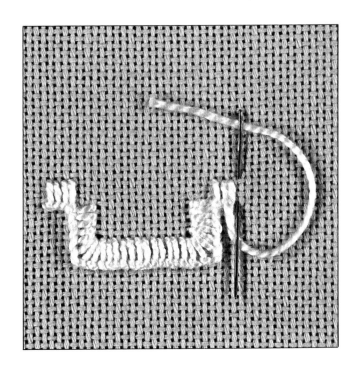

Picots

Bind the groups of threads, taking your needle under the first two threads of the bar and over each pair of threads in the bar four times. You should now be in the centre of the bar. Now make one chain-stitch in the middle of the bar, over the two threads. In the loop of

the chain-stitch, embroider a further chain-stitch to make a clear knot. Work another little knot on the opposite side of the bar and finish off the bar by binding it four more times.

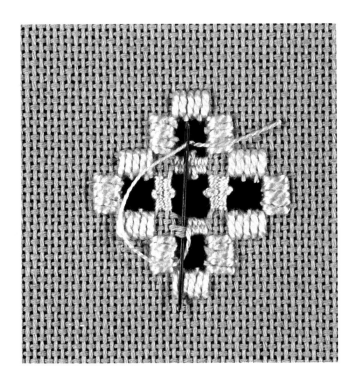

Hems ⊹ ⊹ ⊹ ⊹ ⊹ ⊹ ⊹ ⊹ ⊹

When you are buying material, allow an extra 11cm (4in) for a double hem 3cm (1in) wide. Allow an extra 10–15cm (4–6in) material on top of that for safety's sake.

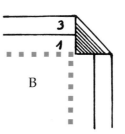

1 = Upper side
2 = Inner side
3 = Turn-in

Double hems

For this example we are using Davosa 3770 or Carrara 3969 material.

In the charts, a dotted line always indicates the double hem, showing the distance from the embroidery. This is where you pull out *one* thread of the weave from side to side. Cut off the rest of the material thirty-six threads beyond this hem line.

Now, following diagram A, mark twelve threads each for the upper side (1), inner side (2) and the turned-in part (3). Fold over the turn-ins and then fold the corner into the corner of the hem lines and cut off the hatched part (diagram B).

Then, following diagram C, turn over the inner side of the hem and sew it down using hem stitch. Close the mitred corner seam with small stitches.

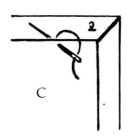

Hemstitch

This stitch is worked from left to right using two strands of embroidery twist or No. 16 four-ply embroidery thread.

Following the line of the pulled thread, take two threads alternately from either side of the line and then stitch vertically, two threads down, into the double hem.

Tablecloths

Cutting out

First of all, cut off the selvedges – these would go out of shape when you washed the cloth.

Round tablecloth

Cut the cloth into a square: the diameter of the tablecloth should be the length of one side of the square.

Use a piece of string or non-stretch cord, the length of which should be the radius of the tablecloth, as a pair of compasses, as follows: knot the ends of the string and mark the centre of the tablecloth with a pin. Then put one loop of string around the pin and put a pencil in the other. Finally, keeping the string taut, draw your circle. This is the line you will cut along.

How to fold the material

1. Fold the material twice. This represents a quarter of the tablecloth. Pin the open edges together so that the layers of fabric will not slip when you are cutting.

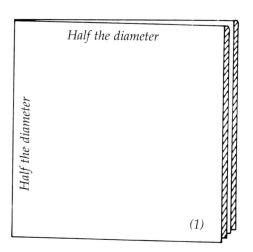

2. Draw a quarter-circle as described above, then cut along the line, cutting through all four layers of material at the same time with sharp dressmakers' scissors.

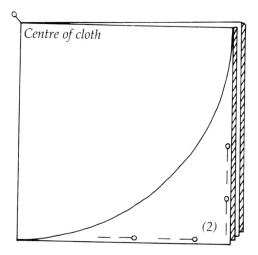

Oval tablecloth

Cut the material into a rectangle and fold it once. Pin the edges together to stop the layers of fabric slipping.

Measure off half the width of the tablecloth from both sides and mark the places on the fold, using pins. These points mark the centres of each semi-circle – the curves at each end of the oval. Mark off the curves in the same way as you did for the round tablecloth. The string is the same length as the width of the folded tablecloth.

Finally, cut along the two curved lines, cutting through both layers of material at once.

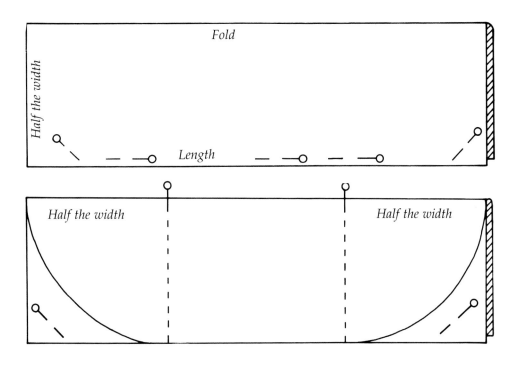

Edging

A finishing touch for your work could be a border of lace, braid or broderie anglaise.

How to work out how much you will need

When you are calculating how much lace edging or braid you will need for your tablecloth, the measurements of the cloth alone will not be enough: you will need some extra for the corners. The amount to add on depends on the width of the lace.

These 'formulas' will give you the exact amount of lace you will need. However, the ends of the lace will overlap slightly, so, for safety's sake, always allow an extra couple of centimetres (about an inch).

Rectangular tablecloth

2 x length of tablecloth + 2 x width of tablecloth + 8 x width of lace = length of lace required.

Round tablecloth

Diameter of tablecloth + 2 x width of lace = overall diameter.
Overall diameter x 3.14 = length of lace required.

Oval tablecloth

Width of tablecloth + 2 x width of lace = overall width.
Overall width x 3.14 = extent of curved areas (two semi-circles).
Length of tablecloth - width of tablecloth = length of middle section.
Extent of curved sections + 2 x length of middle section = length of lace required.

Sewing on edging and lace

First tidy up the cut edges. For round and oval tablecloths, pin or tack the lace all round the cloth (without stretching it) and sew down the ends neatly over each other.

For rectangular and square cloths, pin the lace in the corners at right angles to make a little triangular fold, as shown in diagram 1.

Pin the folds on the wrong side, sew them down and iron them out flat (see diagram 2). Alternatively, with firm, fine lace that will not fray, you can cut the fold off altogether and tidy up the corner (diagram 3).

On the right side, sew the lace on.

1. Right side

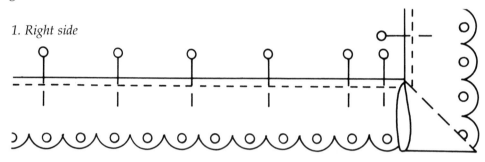

2. Wrong side

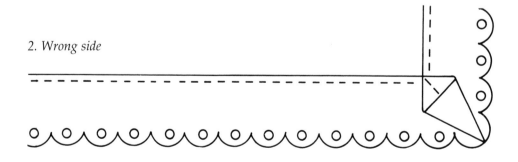

3. Wrong side

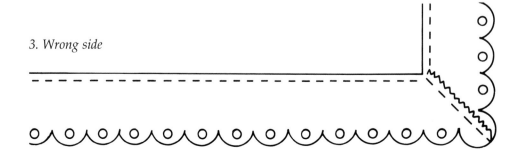

Types of fabric

The aim of this section is to help you choose the right material, because the look of the article is so important. The character of the finished work is determined by not only the embroidery but also the character of the fabric. Smooth, raised, or delicate; coarse or fine; rustic or elegant . . . the fabric and the embroidery form a unified whole, and you will find that using a different fabric will alter the appearance of the stitches.

Also, so that your embroidery will last, you should decide what the item will be used for *before* you choose the appropriate fabric. Are you looking for material to make something useful which is going to be washed a lot, or to make a mat that is purely decorative? Will you be framing your embroidery like a picture or hanging it in the window for the sun to shine through? Or do you want to make a quick personalised greetings card? You can find the right material for anything you want to do.

Choose the right colour for an under-cloth, because this will be visible through the holes in the embroidery: for example, a coloured tablecloth under a runner or top cloth, or toning or contrasting ticking under a Hardanger cushion cover.

The rule of thumb is (no matter whether the fabric is coarse or fine): the denser and closer-woven the fabric is, the better it will wear when used for openwork. The best types, therefore, from coarse to fine, are Davosa, Bellana, Lugana, Meran, Annabelle and Belfast. If you want an open look and are not worried about the work's being hard-wearing, coarse linen is a lovely material.

Apart from the proposed use, it is important to think about how much time you want to spend on your embroidery. This depends not only on the size you want your work to be but also to a considerable extent on the thread-count of the material. For large, magnificent tablecloths and small, quick-to-do presents, fabrics of seven to eight threads to the centimetre (18–20 threads to the inch) are suitable, while someone with a lot of experience in Hardanger work will go for a density of around ten threads to the centimetre (twenty-five threads to the inch).

The charts in this book can be used for all densities of threads, but of course the size of the finished motifs will then vary. So we have given the thread-count for all types of fabric in ten centimetres (and threads per inch). Divide it by four and you will get the number of squares in the chart. To help you convert, in each section on different fabrics you will find the number of squares for the chart. If you use a weave with a higher thread-count than the original, you can repeat a pattern as often as you want, or put in extra motifs, and you will still end up with a similar-sized article. Creative imagination knows no bounds!

This selection of fabrics is also intended to show you that Hardanger, and counted-thread work in general, cannot be worked on just any old material, because the main characteristic of counted-thread fabrics is that they are woven 'square'; in other words, the warp and weft have the same number of threads to the centimetre or inch. This is important, so that borders are the same width in both directions and pattern blocks are the same length. With individual motifs, it is essential that they really do turn out square.

Now you can move on to choosing your material. You will find the appropriate embroidery thread for each type in the table on page 20. Choosing which one to go for is part of the fun of embroidery!

All the fabrics mentioned in this book are manufactured by Zweigart. All the embroidery threads quoted are DMC threads. Equivalent fabrics of a similar thread-count or density and other threads can equally well be used.

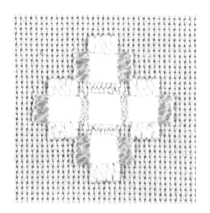 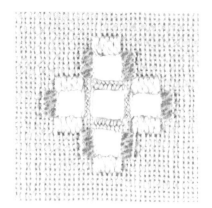

Davosa 3770

- 71 threads = 10cm (18 threads to the inch)
- Available 140cm (55in) and 180cm (71in) wide
- 100 per cent cotton
- Easy care
- Washing instructions: light colours 95°C (203°F), dark colours 60°C (140°F)
- Ironing instructions: • • •

Davosa is a pure-cotton needle-work fabric. Its weave consists of single threads which have been twisted together many times, making them smooth and even and giving the weave its clear, regular look. It is particularly easy to count and because of this it is often recommended by people teaching Hardanger courses. For your first piece of Hardanger it would be the ideal basic material on which to learn the technique. Hardanger experts swear by this material, too, because the work just whizzes along. Lastly, the great choice of colours adds to its popularity.

Ariosa 3711

- 75 threads = 10cm (20 threads to the inch)
- Available 140cm (55in) and 180cm (71in) wide
- 60 per cent viscose, 40 per cent cotton
- Easy care
- Washing instructions: 60°C (140°F)
- Ironing instructions: • • •

The special characteristic of *Ariosa* is its 'flame' twist, created by putting matte cotton 'flame' with shiny viscose. Despite the 'flame' twist the weave is easily counted.

Ariosa is also exceptionally suitable for work which you do not intend to cover with embroidery, where the structure of the weave helps the overall appearance. *Ariosa* is only slightly less densely woven than *Davosa*, so all measurements for *Davosa* on the charts will be pretty much valid for this material too.

Regular, smooth pieces of work get a more rustic touch with *Ariosa*.

Floba 1198

- 69 threads = 10cm (18 threads to the inch)
- Available 140cm (55in) and 170cm (67in) wide
- 70 per cent viscose, 30 per cent linen
- Easy care
- Washing instructions: 60°C (140°F)
- Ironing instructions: • • •

Floba is a counted-thread material made of a viscose/linen mix. Adding linen fibres in the spinning process gives this fabric, with its fluffy fibres, the unmistakable character of natural linen, while the viscose content gives the material a shine. Hardanger open-work looks good contrasted with the natural character of *Floba*.

The thread density is very similar to that of *Davosa*, so you can use the instructions for that material.

To keep your work in top condition, use only detergents for fine fabric, without added bleach or optical brighteners, or the colour of the raw linen fibres may fade.

---

10 squares on the chart = about 56mm (2¼in)

10cm (4in) of the fabric = about 18 squares

---

10 squares on the chart = about 53mm (2in)

10cm (4in) of the fabric = about 19 squares

---

10 squares on the chart = about 58mm (2¼in)

10cm (4in) of the fabric = about 17 squares

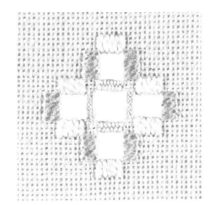

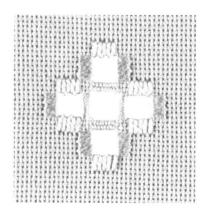

Carrara 3969

- 71 threads = 10cm (18 threads to the inch)
- Available 140cm (55in) wide
- 100 per cent polyacrylic
- Washing instructions: 30°C (86°F)
- Ironing instructions: •

Cork 3613

- 73 threads = 10cm (19 threads to the inch)
- Available 140cm (55in) wide
- 100 per cent pure linen
- Washing instructions: 95°C (203°F)
- Ironing instructions: • • •

Bellana 3256

- 80 threads = 10cm (20 threads to the inch)
- Available 140cm (55in) and 180cm (71in) wide
- 52 per cent cotton, 48 per cent viscose
- Washing instructions: 60°C (140°F)
- Ironing instructions: • • •

Carrara, like *Davosa*, is a smooth, regular fabric made of thread that has been twisted many times. The densities of the threads are identical, so you can use all the *Davosa* charts without any alteration when you are working on *Carrara*.

The only real difference is in what the fibres are made of. If you particularly want a fabric to be easy-care, this is the one for you: it is completely synthetic. The only thing to remember is that the washing temperature must not exceed 30°C (86°F). The material stays the same, and if you should happen to use gold or silver embroidery threads, you will not have any problems.

Cork is a particularly good material. It is also known as coarse or heavy linen. The open weave ensures that the linen structure and smooth, gently gleaming flax thread are shown to their full advantage. Its transparency, when accompanied by Hardanger embroidery, means that this material never looks coarse, despite its relatively low thread-density.

You should not make castellated edges from this material, and do not make anything you want to be hard-wearing; you will find other materials more suitable.

Bellana is a pearly fabric which is especially easy to count. Multi-twist threads with viscose give it a smooth, beautifully shiny appearance and a visible weave structure.

Its thread count is somewhere between those of *Davosa* and *Lugana*, so it looks finer than the former but does not require such intensive work. Even Hardanger-lovers who know the technique well often appreciate the fact that embroidery takes less time on *Bellana*, even for large items. It is also good for combining with cross-stitch, because cross-stitch over two threads looks so delicate.

You can also buy *Bellana* in gold or silver for Christmas embroidery, but only wash this at 30°C (86°F).

10 squares on the chart = about 56mm (2¼in)

10 cm (4in) of the fabric = about 18 squares

10 squares on the chart = about 53mm (2in)

10cm (4in) of the fabric = about 19 squares.

10 squares on the chart = about 50mm (2in)

10cm (4in) of the fabric = about 20 squares

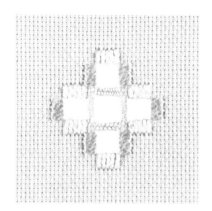

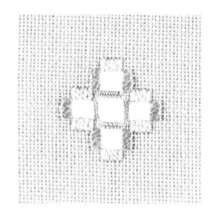

Oslo 3947

- 87 'stitches' of the weave = 10cm (22 threads to the inch)
- Available 170cm (67in) wide
- 100 per cent cotton
- Mercerised; easy care
- Washing instructions: light colours 95°C (203°F), dark colours 60°C (140°F)
- Ironing instructions: ••••

Oslo has the traditional Scandinavian Hardanger structure and therefore is often labelled 'Hardanger fabric'. It has the so-called Panama bond in which the threads cross in pairs. These pairs of threads are called a 'stitches', and when counting a stitch is treated as a single thread.

The material actually has a count of around 175 thin threads to 10cm (4in), which makes it look fine, and yet it is still as easy to count as the coarser weaves. *Oslo* also has a shine and keeps its colour beautifully because of its mercerised-cotton content.

Lugana 3835

- 100 threads = 10cm (25 threads to the inch)
- Available 140cm (55in) and 170cm (67in) wide
- 52 per cent cotton, 48 per cent viscose
- Easy care
- Washing instructions: 60°C (140°F)
- Ironing instructions: ••••

Lugana is a fine, smooth material with a round three-ply twisted thread which gives it a pearly surface; despite its high density it is easy to count. The viscose content means that it has a soft shine.

With ten threads to the centimetre (twenty-five threads to the inch) we are now coming to the realms of the practised Hardanger embroiderer who is prepared to invest a bit more time in creating something fine and delicate. Working on *Lugana* is not actually any more difficult; the technique is just the same and *anyone* can manage a coaster or a greetings card, not just the professionals.

Dublin 3604

- 100 threads = 10cm (25 threads to the inch)
- Available 140cm (55in) and 170cm (67in) wide
- 100 per cent pure linen
- Washing instructions: 95°C (203°F)
- Ironing instructions: ••••

Dublin is the classic linen: it is the fine counterpart of *Cork*. Its open weave of smooth, high-quality flax threads, finely spun, looks delicate and transparent. When you work Hardanger embroidery on it, the result is something rather special.

As with *Cork*, avoid castellated edges. If, however, you are prepared to be especially careful with your embroidery, you could try the extra-reinforced castellated edge described on page 10.

---

10 squares on the chart = about 46mm (1³/₄ in)

10cm (4in) of the fabric = about 22 squares

---

10 squares on the chart = about 40mm (1³/₄ in)

10cm (4in) of the fabric = about 25 squares

---

10 squares on the chart = about 40mm (1³/₄ in)

10cm (4in) of the fabric = about 25 squares

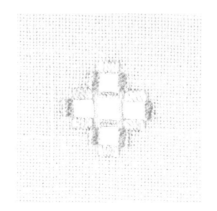

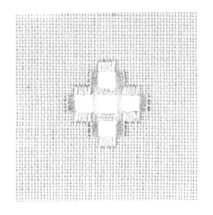

Meran 3972

- 107 threads = 10cm (28 threads to the inch)
- Available 140cm (55in) and 180cm (71in) wide
- 60 per cent viscose, 40 per cent cotton
- Easy care
- Washing instructions: 60°C (140°F)
- Ironing instructions: • • •

Meran, like *Ariosa*, consists of a matte cotton 'flame' twisted together with shiny viscose. The fabric is finer and more faceted, but makes just as strong an impression and is equally unmistakable.

As with *Ariosa*, the combination of the delicate embroidery and the textured weave means that there does not have to be masses of embroidery to get a decorative effect. You can get both *Meran* and *Ariosa* in fashion colours, so you can give a traditional embroidery an up-to-the-minute touch.

Annabelle 3240

- 112 threads = 10cm (28 threads to the inch)
- Available 140cm (55in) and 180cm (71in) wide
- 100 per cent cotton
- Easy care
- Washing instructions: 60°C (140°F)
- Ironing instructions: • • •

Annabelle is a fine, densely woven textured fabric made of pure cotton. It is enlivened by weak 'flames' some distance apart, and this keeps it even and easily counted.

It has the character of linen with the easy-care properties of pure cotton and is therefore easier to iron. If you love doing very fine Hardanger work, this is the perfect material for you.

Belfast 3609

- 122 threads = 10cm (32 threads to the inch)
- Available 140cm (55in) wide
- 100 per cent pure linen
- Washing instructions: 95°C (203°F)
- Ironing instructions: • • •

Belfast is a fine, smooth, pure-linen material made from long-fibred flax threads, closely woven yet still easy to count. Of all the fabrics discussed here, it is probably the finest and most beautiful, and expert Hardanger embroiderers will find it the perfect material on which to create an embroidered work of art.

If the material gets any finer than this, counting gets more difficult and the basic Hardanger block should be increased from four to six threads.

---

10 squares on the chart = about 37mm (1½in)

10cm (4in) of the fabric = about 27 squares

---

10 squares on the chart = about 36mm (1½in)

10cm (4in) of the fabric = about 28 squares

---

10 squares on the chart = about 33mm (1¼in)

10cm (4in) of the fabric = about 31 squares

Hardanger fabrics at a glance

Thickness of thread	Fabric*	DMC embroidery thread to use	Needle size
7 threads to the centimetre (18 threads to the inch)	Floba 1198 Davosa 3770 Carrara 3969	Satin stitch: Pearl No. 3	No. 20
7.5 threads to the centimetre (20 threads to the inch)	Ariosa 3711 Cork 3613	Overcasting: Pearl No. 5 Pearl No. 8	Nos. 20 or 22 Nos. 22 or 24
8 threads to the centimetre (20 threads to the inch)	Bellana 3256	Satin stitch: Pearl No. 5	Nos. 20 or 22
9 threads to the centimetre (22 threads to the inch)	Oslo 3947		
10 threads to the centimetre (25 threads to the inch)	Lugana 3835 Dublin 3604	Overcasting: Pearl No. 8	Nos. 22 or 24
11 threads to the centimetre (28 threads to the inch)	Meran 3972 Annabelle 3240		
12 threads to the centimetre (32 threads to the inch)	Belfast 3609	Satin stitch: Pearl No. 8 Overcasting: 4-ply embroidery thread No. 16	Nos. 22 or 24 No. 24

All fabrics have a name and a reference number, as shown above. Elsewhere in this book the number contains a suffix to denote the colour of the material.

PROJECTS

Cushion covers, bedspread and tablecloth

DAVOSA 3770
Cushion: about 40 x 40cm (16 x 16in)
Bedcover: about 120 x 200cm (47 x 79in)
Tablecloth: about 70 x 70cm (28 x 28in)

EMBROIDERY THREAD
Satin-stitch motifs: Pearl No. 3
Bars: Pearl No. 8, closely overcast

To make it easier for you to follow the pattern, the chart (motifs A and B) is an exact representation of the motifs used. Each quarter of the motif has been photographed and the central stitch has been marked with a dotted line. First establish the middle of the cushion or tablecloth and then, working outwards from that point, lay out the embroidery so that when you have finished there will be borders of equal width left over all round.

Cushion covers

The cushion covers are made by working a motif, either whole or in part; for example, you might use the central motif.

Bedspread

The bedspread is worked in separate sections, each like a cushion cover and 40 x 40cm (16 x 16in) square.

You will need eight panels of motif B without the festoon border and seven panels of motif A. To make up the bedspread, simply sew them together.

To show off the effect properly, put a lining in an appropriate colour beneath the Hardanger work.

Tablecloth

Start with central motif A and extend the diagonal rhomboid shape to each side by one 'lozenge', then embroider the border motif according to the instructions.

The matching undercloth is hemmed with the festoon edging from motif B.

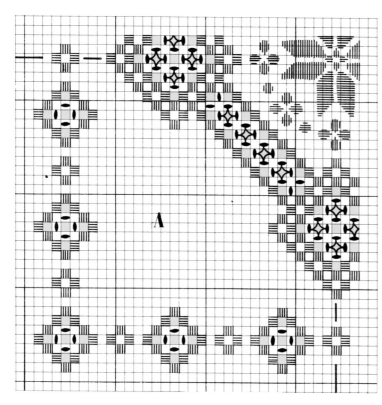

Charts for pages 21 and 26.

Charts A and B each show a quarter of the cushion cover. Chart C shows rather more than a quarter of the yellow tablecloth on page 27.

Always turn the charts by a quarter-turn and set them against the dotted central line.

The Hardanger charts are in blocks of four threads and the detailed drawing for the satin-stitch motifs is shown thread for thread.

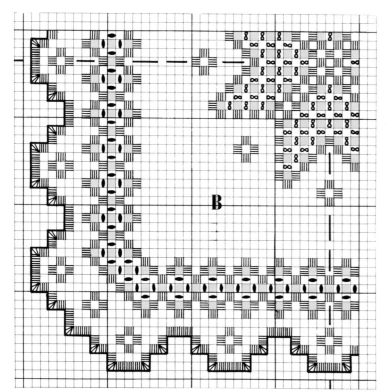

Detail of satin-stitch motif.

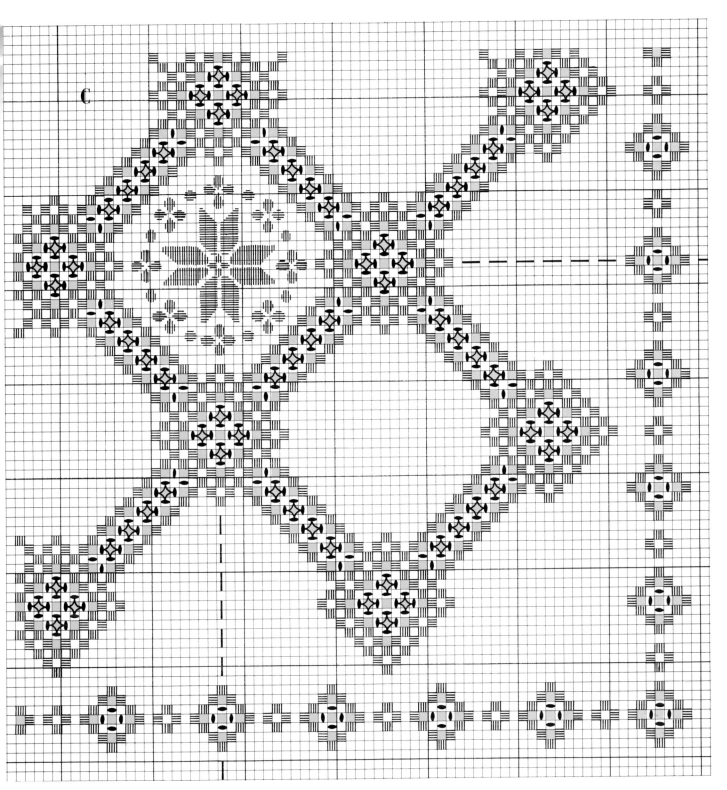

Chart for pages 21 and 27.

Motif A.

Motifs for pages 26 and 27.

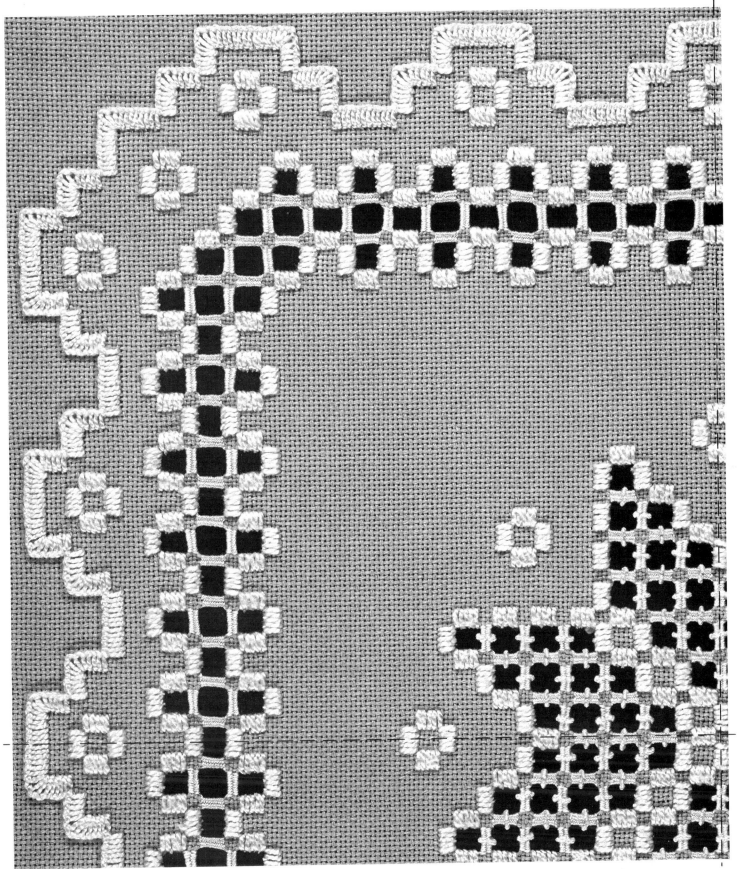

Motif B.

Bedspread and cushion covers.

Yellow tablecloth.

White tablecloth

Davosa 3770/1 or Carrara 3969/11
Size of cloth: about 79 x 79cm (31 x 31in)
Size of fabric: about 90 x 90cm (35 x 35in)

Embroidery thread
Satin-stitch motifs: Pearl No. 3
Overcasting: Pearl No. 3

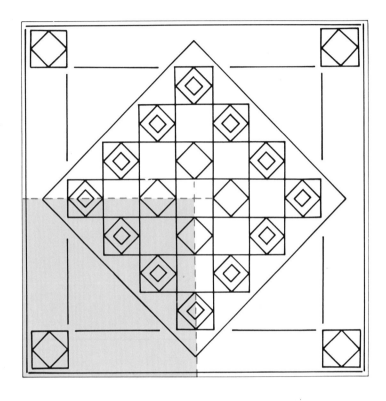

Suggested layout for a tablecloth

Size of cloth: about 120 x 120cm (47 x 47in)

This tablecloth is illustrated on page 2.

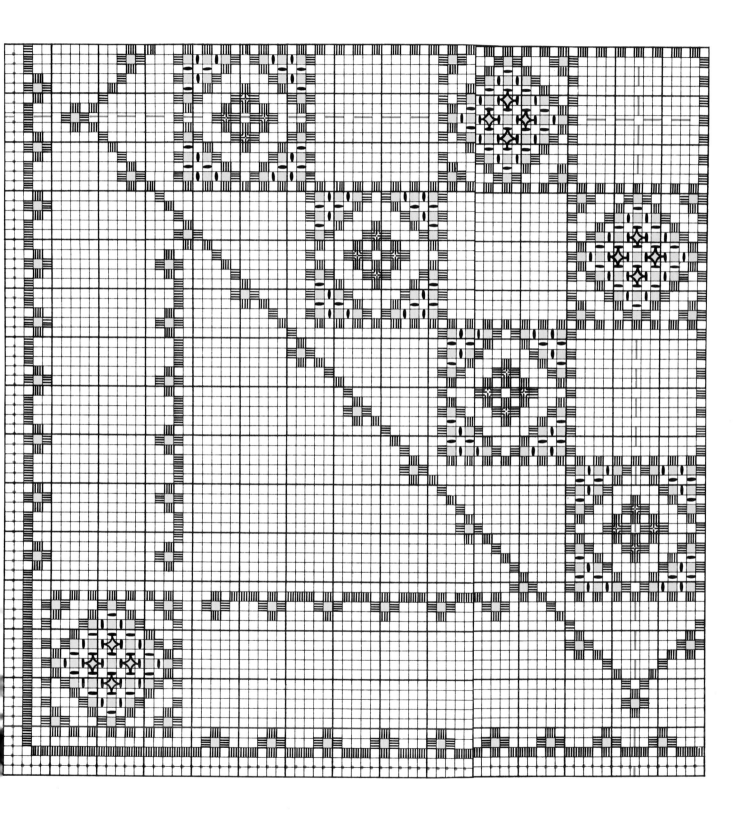

Pink tablecloth

Davosa 3770/449 or Carrara 3969/449
Size of cloth: about 79 x 79cm (31 x 31in)
Size of fabric: about 90 x 90cm (35 x 35in)

Embroidery thread:
Satin-stitch motifs: Pearl No. 3
Overcasting: Pearl No. 8

See also the pink cushion cover on page 48.

You will find the chart on page 32.

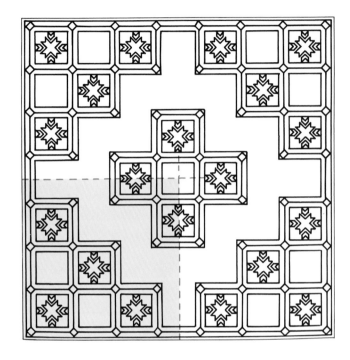

Satin-stitch motif.

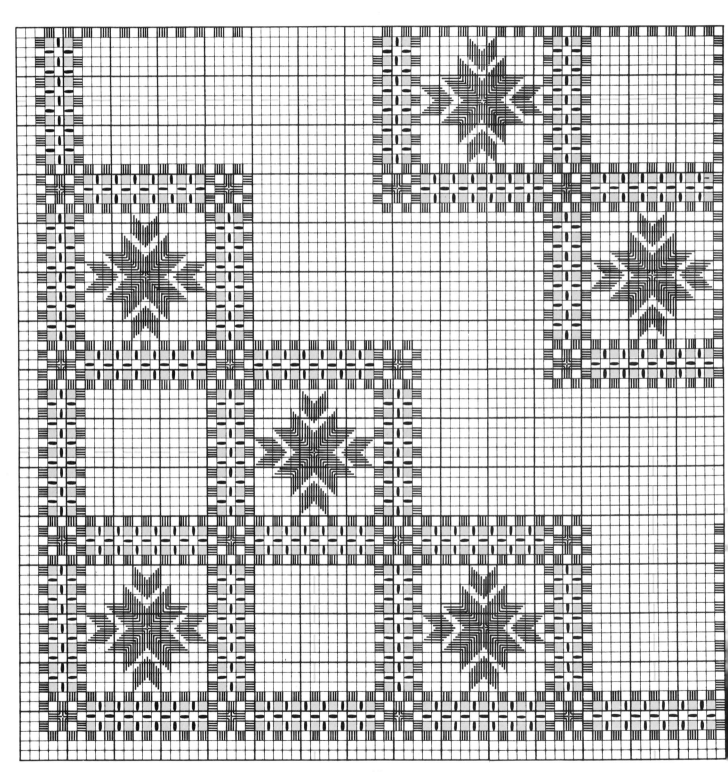

Chart for pages 30 and 31 and the pink cushion cover on page 48.

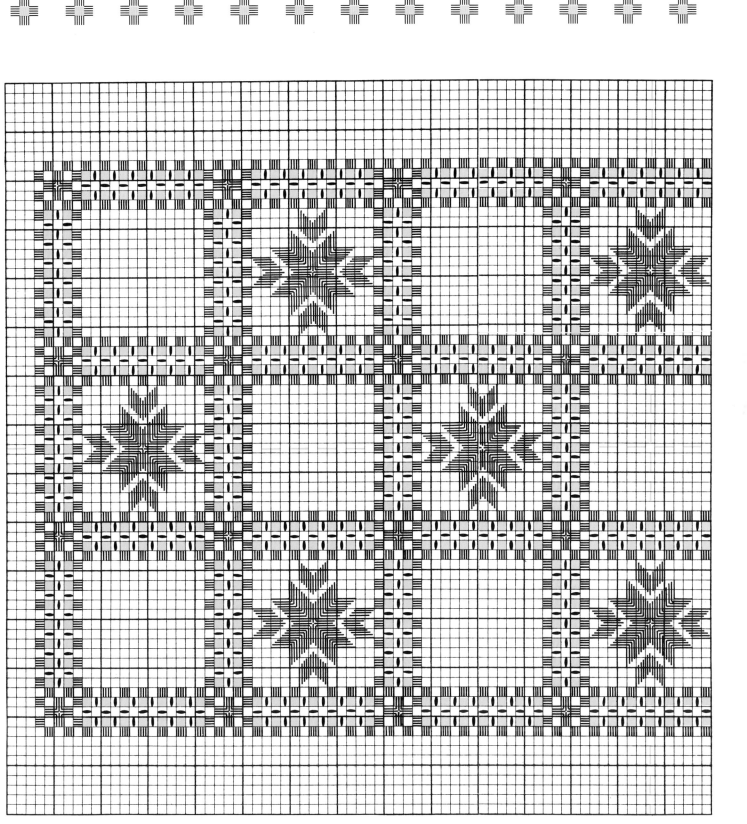

Chart for pages 34 and 35.

White table-runner ✚ ✚ ✚ ✚ ✚

Davosa 3770/1 or Carrara 3969/11
Size of runner: about 38 x 79cm (15 x 31in)
Size of fabric: about 50 x 90cm (20 x 35in)

Embroidery thread
Satin-stitch motifs: Pearl No. 3
Overcasting: Pearl No. 8

The satin-stitch motif is shown thread for thread on page 30.

You will find the chart on page 33.

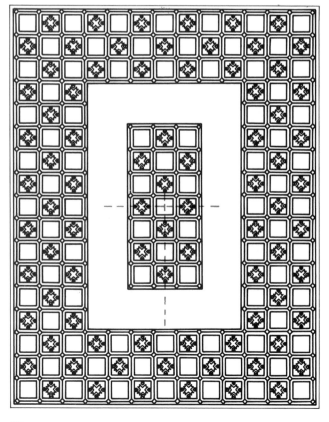

Suggested layout for a tablecloth

Size of embroidery: about 132 x 175cm (52 x 69in)

The central motif matches that of the table-runner. The border embroidery is 124 threads from the central motif block. This corresponds to two motif squares.

White table-runner.

Pink table-runner

Davosa 3770/449 or Carrara 3969/449
Size of runner: about 79 x 42cm (31 x 17in)
Size of fabric: about 90 x 55cm (35 x 22in)

Embroidery thread:
Satin-stitch motifs: Pearl No. 3
Overcasting: Pearl No. 8

> You will find the chart on page 38.

Satin-stitch motif.

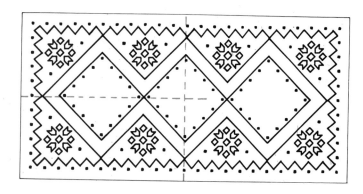

The table-runner can be lengthened at any time by repeating the pattern block (144 threads). This means it will be extended by about 20.5cm (8in) each time.

You will find a suggested layout for a cushion cover on page 47.

Pink table-runner.

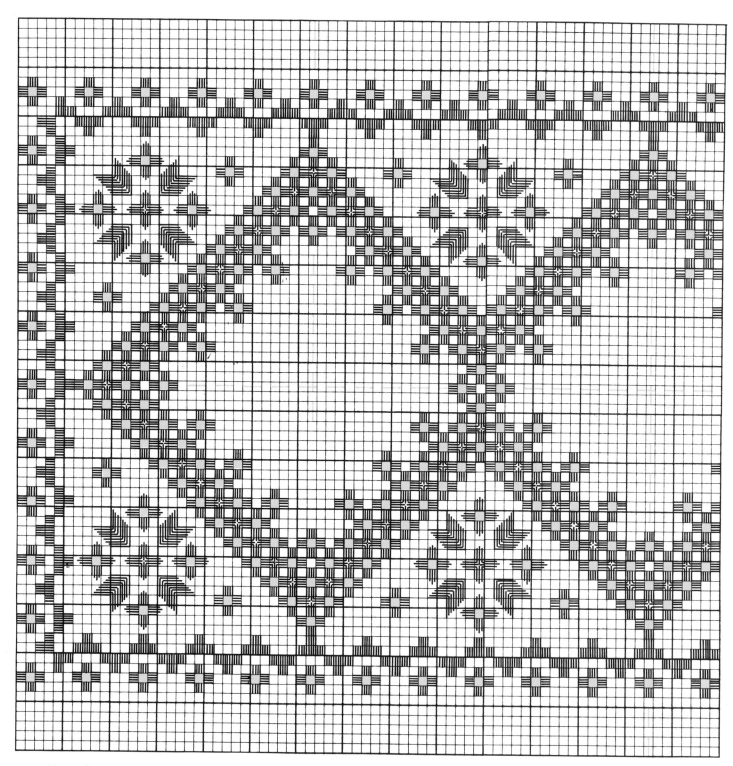

Charts for pages 36 and 37.

Charts for pages 40 and 41.

Beige tablecloth

Davosa 3770/264 or Carrara 3969/52
Size of tablecloth: about 79 x 79cm (31 x 31in)
Size of fabric: about 90 x 90cm (35 x 35in)

EMBROIDERY THREAD
Satin-stitch motifs: Pearl No. 3
Overcasting: Pearl No. 8

You will find the chart on page 39.

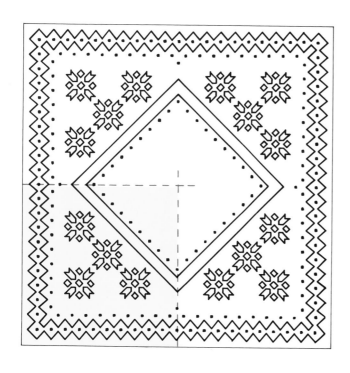

Beige tablecloth.

Small white tablecloth ✚ ✚ ✚ ✚

Davosa 3770/1 or Carrara 3969/11
Size of tablecloth: about 79 x 79cm (31 x 31in)
Size of fabric: about 90 x 90cm (35 x 35in)

Embroidery thread
Satin-stitch motifs: Pearl No. 3
Overcasting: Pearl No. 8

You will find the chart on page 44.

Satin-stitch motif.

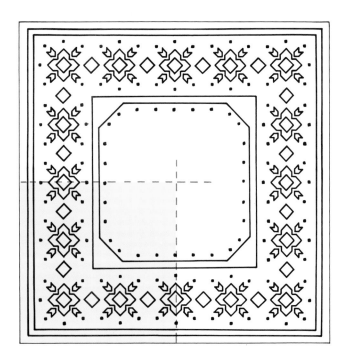

Small white tablecloth.

Chart for pages 42–43.

Chart for the green cushion cover on page 49.

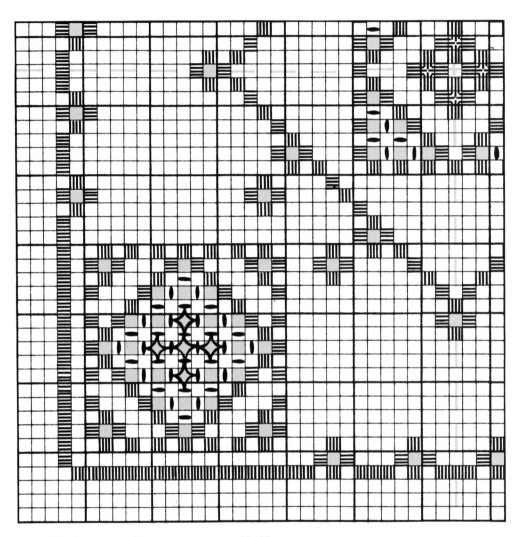

Chart for the grey cushion cover on pages 48–49.

Layout idea for a cushion cover.

Pastel cushion covers

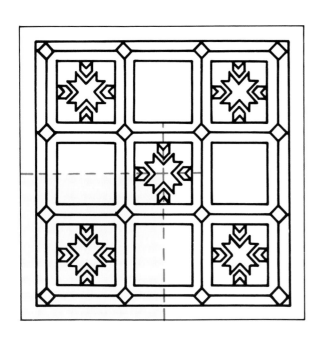

Pink cushion cover

DAVOSA 3770/430 OR CARRARA 3969/430
Size of cushion cover: about 40 x 40cm (16 x 16in)
Size of fabric: about 50 x 90cm (20 x 35in)

EMBROIDERY THREAD
Satin-stitch motifs: Pearl No. 3
Overcasting: Pearl No. 8

The cushion-cover motif corresponds exactly, stitch for stitch, to the left part of the chart on page 32.
   For the satin-stitch motif, see page 30.

Grey cushion cover

DAVOSA 3770/708 OR CARRARA 3969/708
Size of cushion cover: about 40 x 40cm (16 x 16in)
Size of fabric: about 50 x 90cm (20 x 35in)

EMBROIDERY THREAD
Satin-stitch motifs: Pearl No. 3
Overcasting: Pearl No. 8

You will find the chart on page 46.

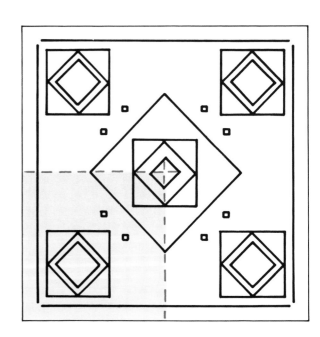

Green cushion cover

DAVOSA 3770/629 OR CARRARA 3969/629
Size of cushion cover: about 40 x 40cm (16 x 16in)
Size of fabric: about 50 x 90cm (20 x 35in)

EMBROIDERY THREAD
Satin-stitch motifs: Pearl No. 3
Overcasting: Pearl No. 8

You will find the chart on page 45.

Roller blind

Meran 3972 or Ariosa 3711

Meran	*Pattern block*: about 20cm (8in)
	Height of border: about 21cm (8¼in)
Ariosa	*Pattern block*: about 28cm (11in)
	Height of border: about 30cm (11¾in)

Embroidery thread

Ariosa	*Satin-stitch motifs*: Pearl No. 3
	Overcasting: Pearl No. 8
Meran	*Satin-stitch motifs*: Pearl No. 5
	Overcasting: Pearl No. 8

You will find the charts on pages 52 and 53.

The original is embroidered on Meran.

The repeat of the pattern block depends on the width of your window. To right and left, even out the design with a lengthened or shortened border, and take the scalloped side borders up as high as you like to tailor the blind to your own window.

Suggested layout for a tablecloth

On the chart, omit the first large flower and only embroider the curve. Turn the chart by 90° and put it in the corner in the pattern. Work the corner as in the roller blind. The size of the tablecloth can be increased by repeating pattern blocks – 20cm (8in) each time on Meran and 28cm (11in) on Ariosa.

Scalloped border

Meran	Pearl No. 8
Ariosa	Pearl No. 5

After you have finished the Hardanger work, cast off the fabric twelve threads from the edge. Only cut off a little at a time, so the edge does not fray before it has been secured.

Turn in the cut edge to a depth of four threads and start the scalloped border as shown in the sketch: alternate five stitches over four threads and three stitches over eight threads, to fit into the Hardanger holes. At the corners, work five scallop stitches into the same point of entry.

Suggested layout for a tablecloth.

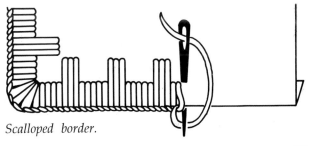

Scalloped border.

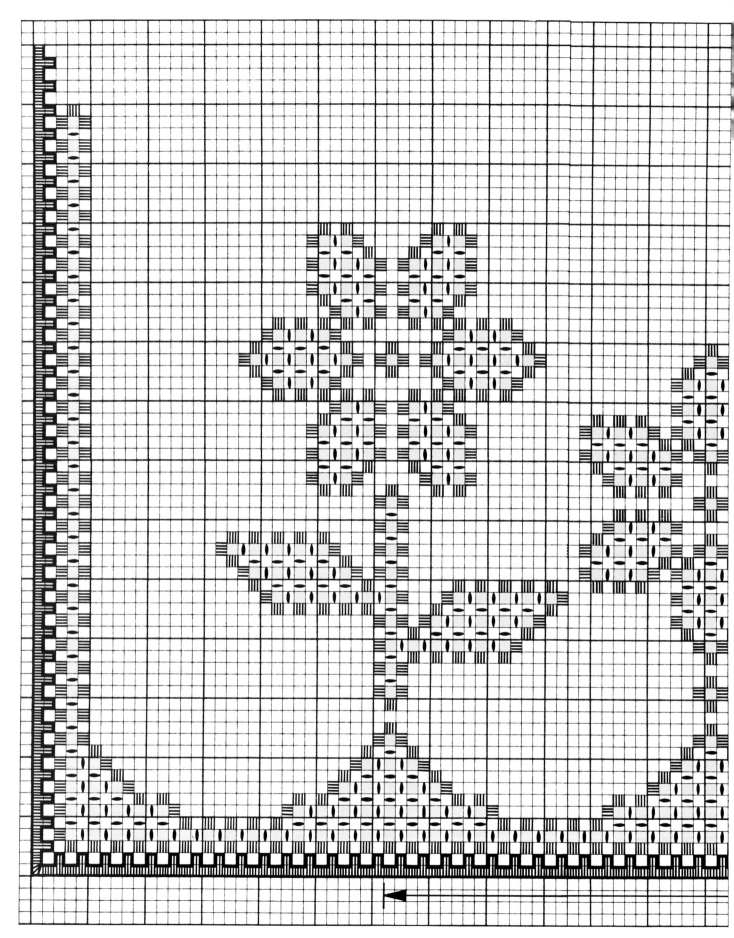

Chart for pages 50–51.

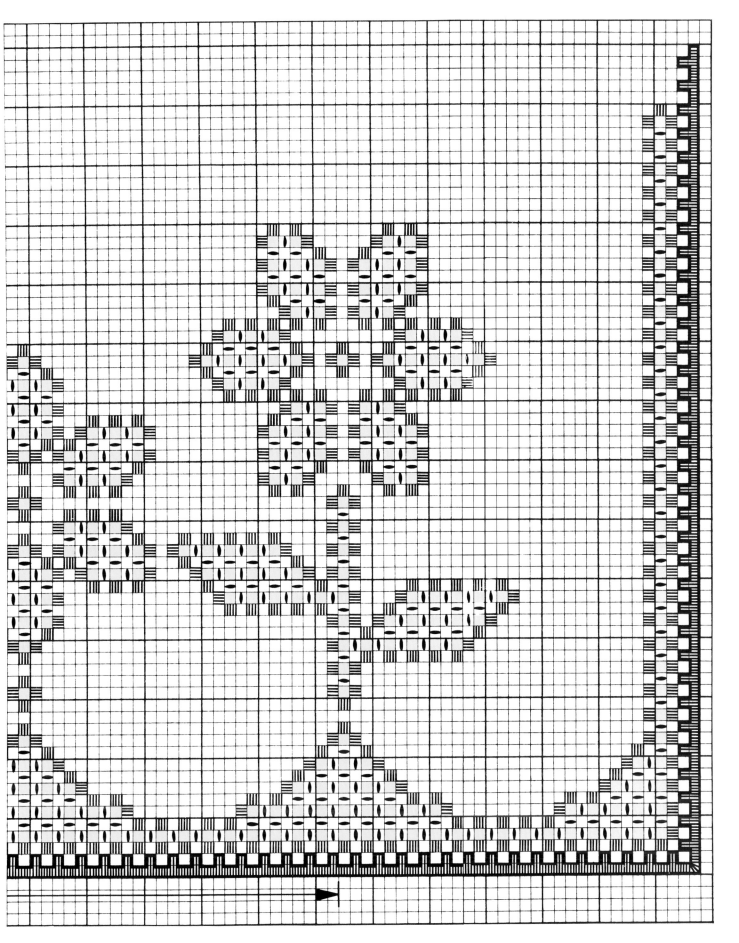

'Flowers on lace' tablecloth ⊞ ⊞ ⊞

ARIOSA 3711

Size of embroidered panel: about 89 x 89cm (35 x 35in)

MERAN 3972

Size of embroidered panel: about 62 x 62cm (24 x 24in)
The original pattern is embroidered on Ariosa – the finished size of the piece is about 95 x 95cm (37 x 37in) and the size of the fabric is around 105 x 105cm (41 x 41in).

EMBROIDERY THREAD

Ariosa *Satin-stitch motifs*: Pearl No. 3
          Overcasting: Pearl No. 8
Meran   *Satin-stitch motifs*: Pearl No. 5
          Overcasting: Pearl No. 8

The dotted line shows the centre of the tablecloth. Lay out the flower motifs according to the diagram.

The pattern blocks in the area between the two arrows can be repeated as often as you like if you want to make a bigger cloth. The block is 17cm (7in) on Ariosa and about 12cm (5in) on Meran. The hem line is twenty-four threads from the edge of the embroidery. (See page 11 for details of how to sew the double hem.)

You will find the chart on pages 56 and 57.

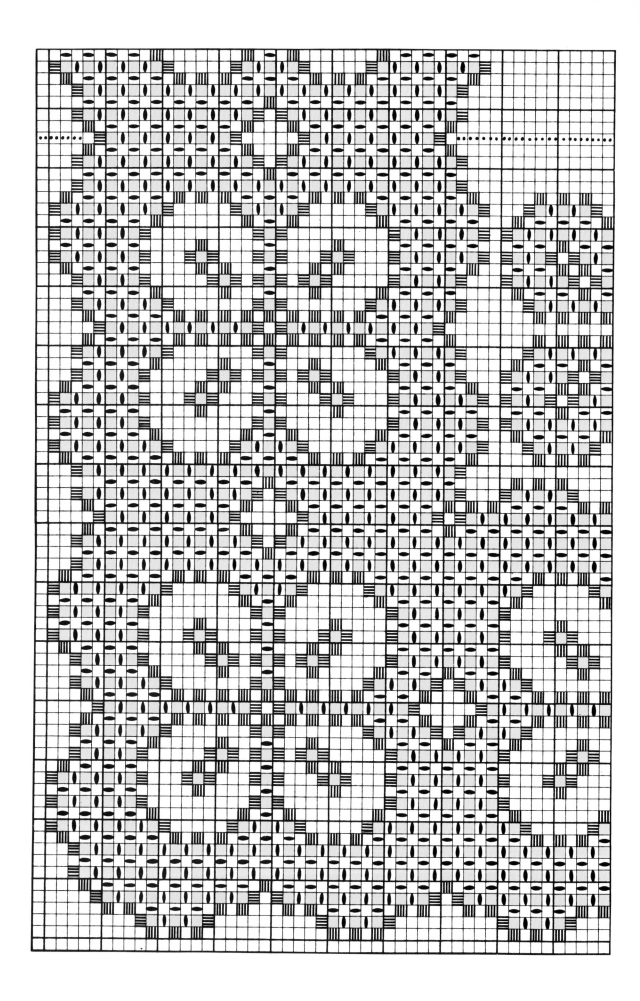

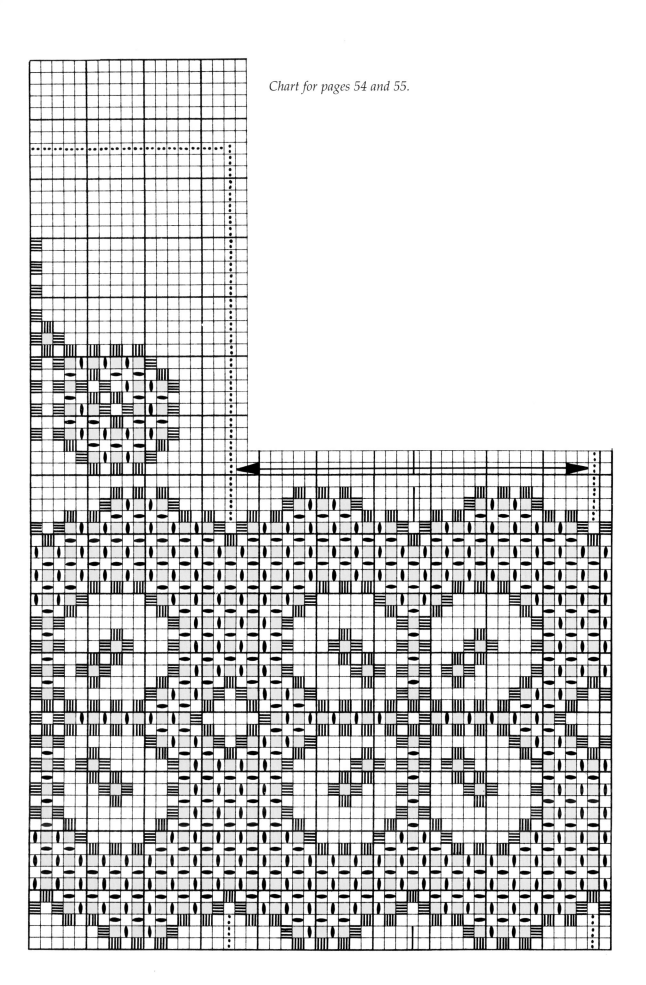

Chart for pages 54 and 55.

Heart-motif window picture

MERAN 3972
Diameter: about 27cm (10½in)
Fabric required: about 37 x 37cm (14½ x 14½in)
ARIOSA 3711
Diameter: about 39cm (15½in)
Fabric required: about 49 x 49cm (19 x 19in)

EMBROIDERY THREAD
Ariosa *Satin-stitch motifs*: Pearl No. 3
Overcasting: Pearl No. 8
Meran *Satin-stitch motifs*: Pearl No. 5
Overcasting: Pearl No. 8

The original was embroidered on Meran. The size depends on the rings you can buy in your needlecraft shop – so buy the ring before you buy your material! The amount of fabric you will need is a square about 10cm (4in) larger than the diameter of your ring.

To use this design for a tablecloth

Embroider the round heart-motif in the middle of the fabric. Then take a thread, double it, and knot it at the length of the radius of the circle you want to draw. Pin one end of the thread to the centre of the motif, insert a pencil in the loop at the other end, and mark out the circle. Then place the rest of the motifs radiating from the centre.

The diameter of the tablecloth is 60cm (24in) for Meran and 85cm (34in) for Ariosa. The diameter of the central motif is 25cm (10in) for Meran and 36cm (14in) for Ariosa.

Round window picture with flower motif

MERAN 3972
Diameter: about 18.5cm (7¼in)
Fabric required: about 28 x 28cm (11 x 11in)

ARIOSA 3711
Diameter: about 26cm (10¼in)
Fabric required: about 36 x 36cm (14 x 14in)

EMBROIDERY THREAD
Ariosa *Satin-stitch motifs*: Pearl No. 3
Overcasting: Pearl No. 8
Meran *Satin-stitch motifs*: Pearl No. 5
Overcasting: Pearl No. 8

You will find the charts on pages 60 and 61.

How to make up the finished piece

Lay the ring on the finished Hardanger motif, and, on the back of the work, draw round the circumference of the ring. Sew a line of zig-zag stitches about 1.5cm (half an inch) from the edge of the material, all the way round, and then cut off the material.

Lay the overhang on to the ring and pin it first at four opposite points and then all the way round (see diagram 1). Working from the front, oversew the ring using alternately a vertical and a diagonal stitch (see diagram 2). Do not pierce the edge of the fabric on the back of the work, but keep on rolling it under the ring.

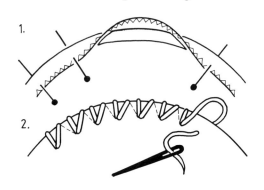

Instructions and chart for the oval window picture are given on pages 62 and 63.

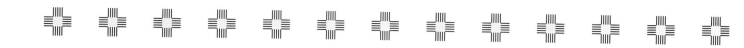

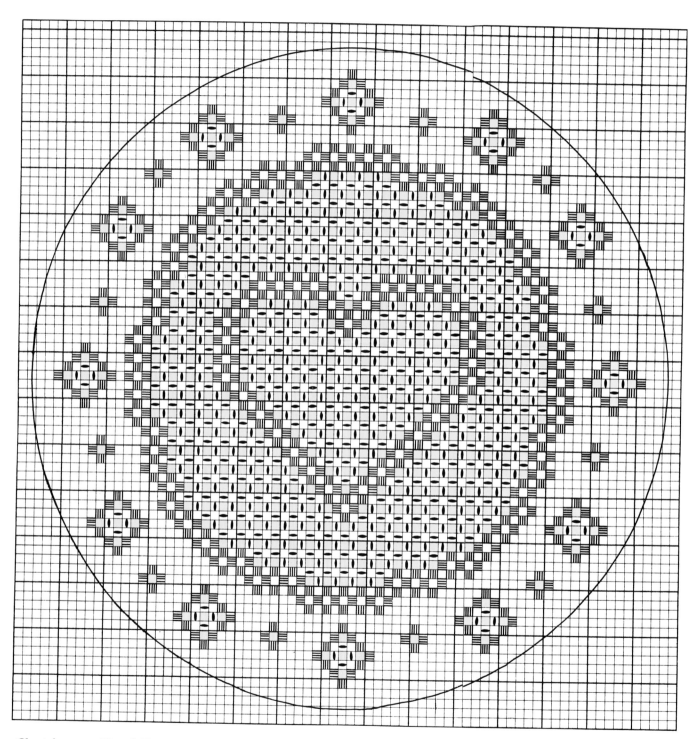

Chart for pages 58 and 59.

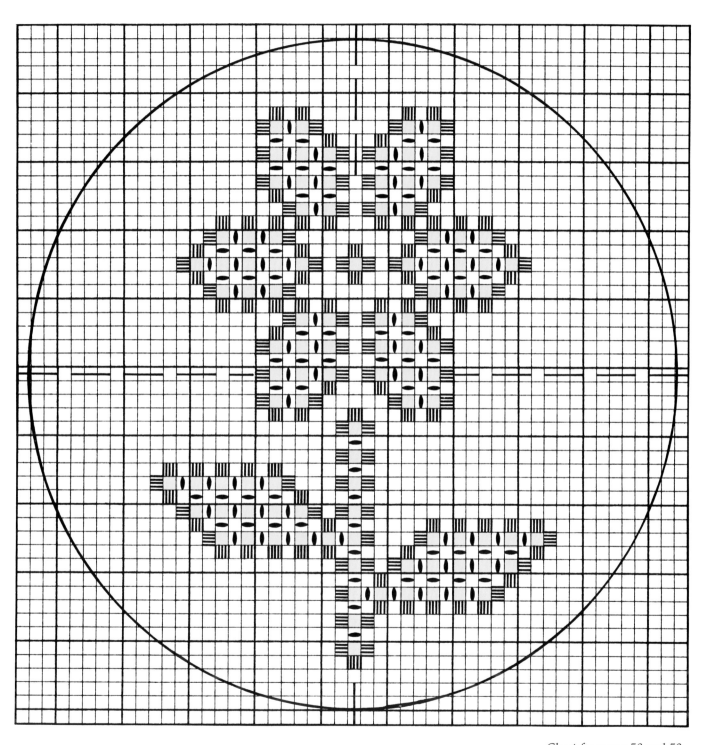

Chart for pages 58 and 59.

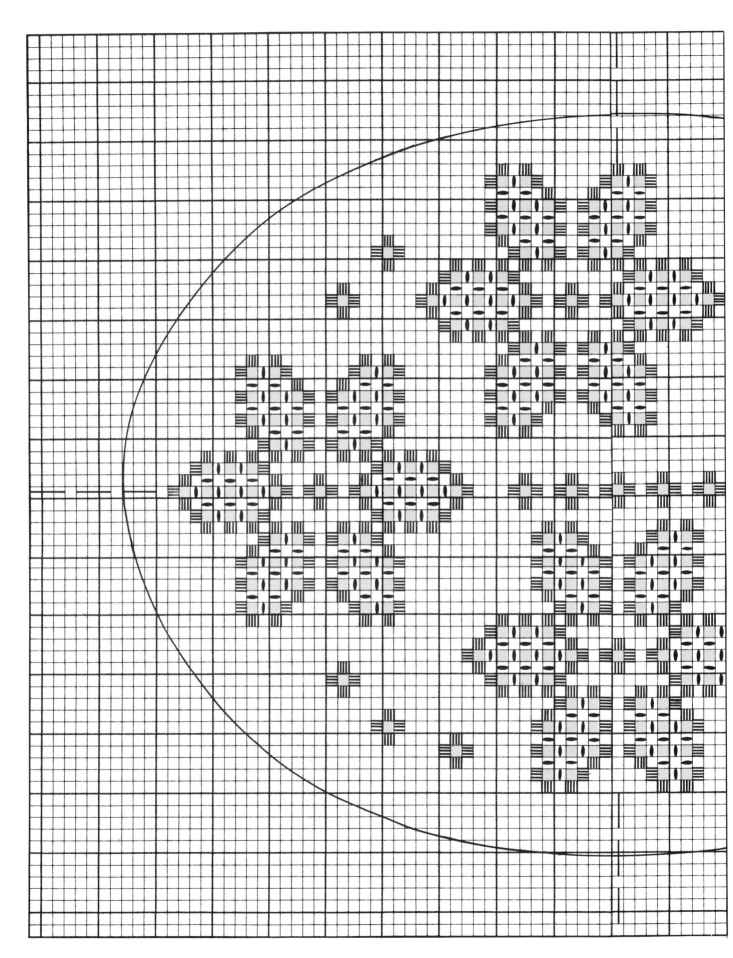

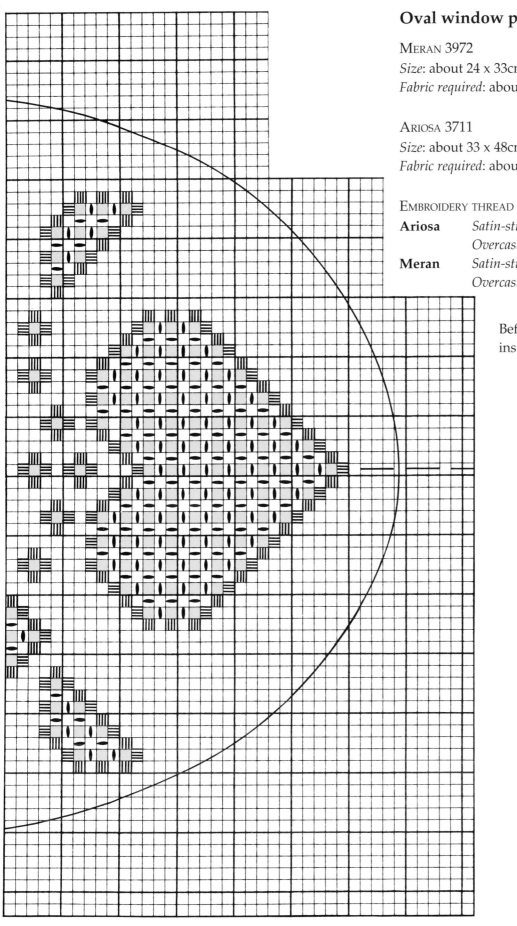

Oval window picture (shown on page 59)

MERAN 3972
Size: about 24 x 33cm (9$\frac{1}{2}$ x 13in)
Fabric required: about 34 and 43cm (13$\frac{1}{2}$ x 17in)

ARIOSA 3711
Size: about 33 x 48cm (13 x 19in)
Fabric required: about 43 x 58cm (17 x 23in)

EMBROIDERY THREAD

Ariosa	*Satin-stitch motifs*: Pearl No. 3	
	Overcasting: Pearl No. 8	
Meran	*Satin-stitch motifs*: Pearl No. 5	
	Overcasting: Pearl No. 8	

Before you start, read the instructions on page 58.

Tablecloth with flowering vine

Ariosa 3711

Size of embroidery: about 80 x 80cm (31½ x 31½in)
Size of finished tablecloth: about 92 x 92cm (36 x 36in)
Size of fabric required: about 105 x 105cm (41x 41in)

Meran 3972

Size of embroidery: about 56 x 56cm (22 x 22in)

The original was embroidered on Ariosa.

The chart gives you further ideas for varying the pattern in the orientation lines that are drawn in.

Embroidery thread

Ariosa	*Satin-stitch motifs*: Pearl No. 3	
	Overcasting: Pearl No. 8	
Meran	*Satin-stitch motifs*: Pearl No. 5	
	Overcasting: Pearl No. 8	

You will find the charts on pages 66 and 67.

The *broken* line marks a quarter of the tablecloth. For the next quarter, turn the chart and place it against the line. The line for the double hem is twenty-eight threads from the edge of the embroidery (for details of how to sew the hem, see page 11).

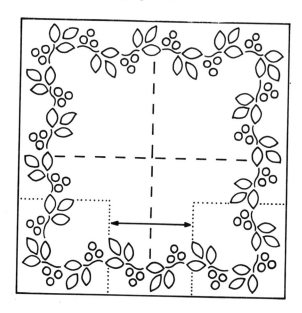

To make a larger tablecloth

The *dotted* line marks off the corners. The section of the pattern between the two arrows can be repeated as often as you like: if you are using Meran it is 18cm (7in) square, and if you are using Ariosa it is 25.5cm (10in).

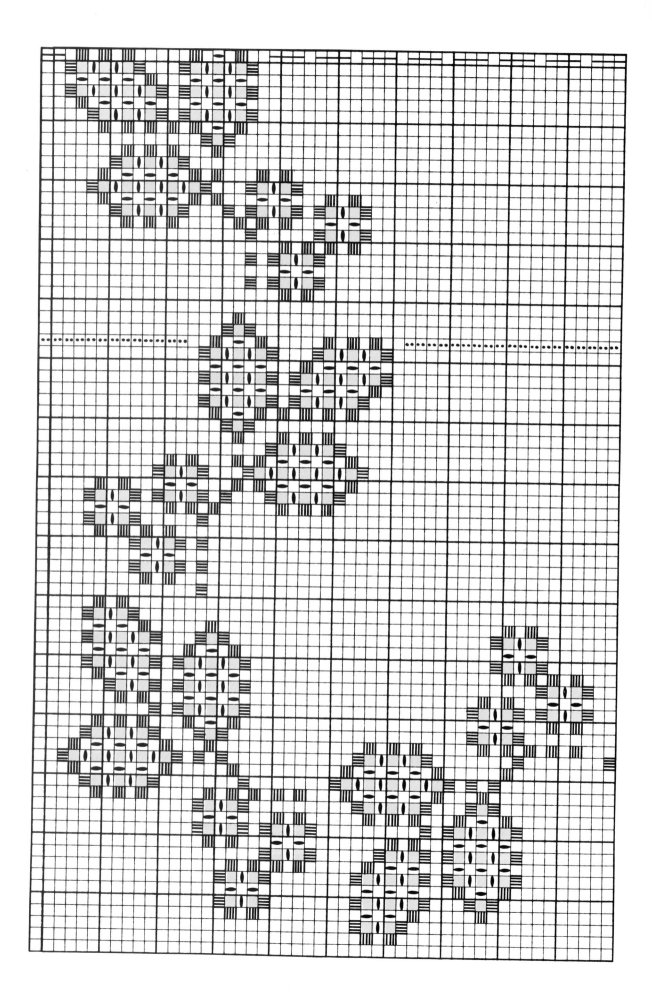

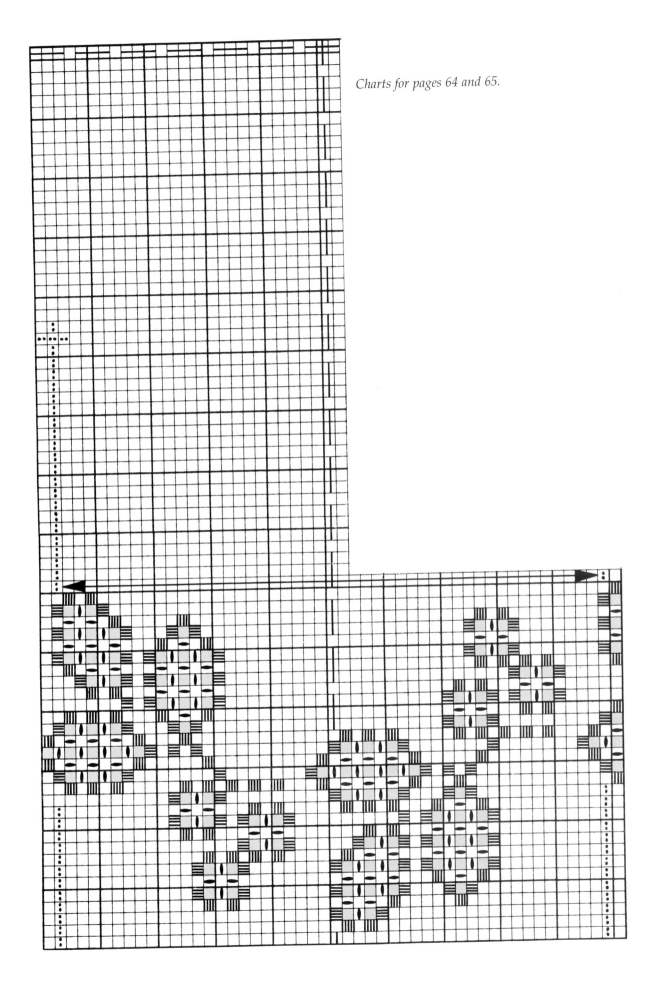

Charts for pages 64 and 65.

Heart-motif mat

MERAN 3972

Size of embroidery: about 25 x 25cm (10 x 10in)

ARIOSA 3711

Size of embroidery: about 36 x 36cm (14 x 14in)

Size including hem: about 41 x 41cm (16 x 16in)

Lacy mat

MERAN 3972

Size of embroidery: about 22 x 22cm (8³/₄ x 8³/₄in)

ARIOSA 3711

Size of embroidery: about 31 x 31cm (12 x 12in)

Size including hem: about 37 x 37cm (14¹/₂ x 14¹/₂in)

EMBROIDERY THREAD

Ariosa *Satin-stitch motifs*: Pearl No. 3
Overcasting: Pearl No. 8

Meran *Satin-stitch motifs*: Pearl No. 5
Overcasting: Pearl No. 8

The originals were embroidered on Ariosa.

The line for the double hem is four threads from the edge of the embroidery. (For details of how to make the hem, see page 11.)

You will find the chart on pages 72 and 73.

More ideas

Here are some more suggested ways of using the embroidery motifs.

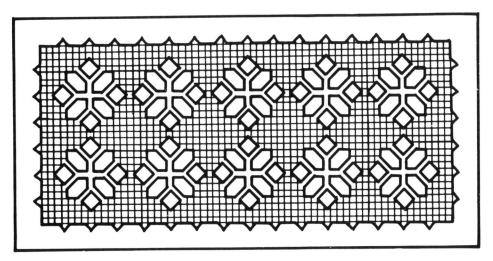

Lacy-mat motif table runner.

To lengthen the runners:

Size of embroidery in the sketch:
Meran: about 22 x 51cm (8³/₄ x 20in)
Ariosa: about 31 x 72cm (12 x 28¹/₄in)

When the motifs are all the same width, repeat the block as often as you like. This will be 9.5cm (3³/₄in) on Meran and 13.5cm (5¹/₄in) on Ariosa.

Put half a motif at each end of the runner and then increase the length of the straight part in between as much as you want.

Heart-motif table runner.

Tablecloth

Arrange the chart from page 72 in a chessboard pattern and in the gaps repeat just the inner motif (the hearts).

You will find the chart on page 72.

Cushion cover

Size of embroidery in the sketch:
Meran: about 32 x 32cm (12½ x 12½in)
Ariosa: about 46 x 46cm (18 x 18in)

> *You will find the chart on page 73.*

The motif is just the right size for a central panel on a cushion cover worked on Ariosa. If you are using Meran you will simply have to extend the latticework.

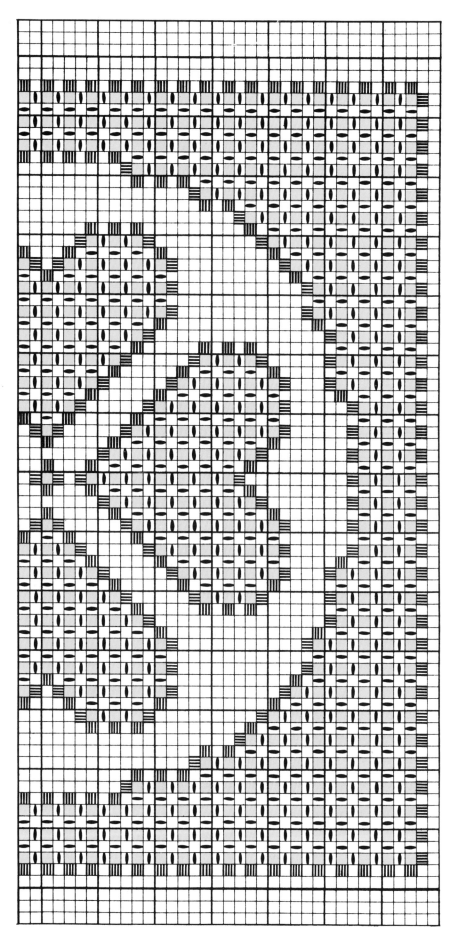

Chart for pages 68–70.

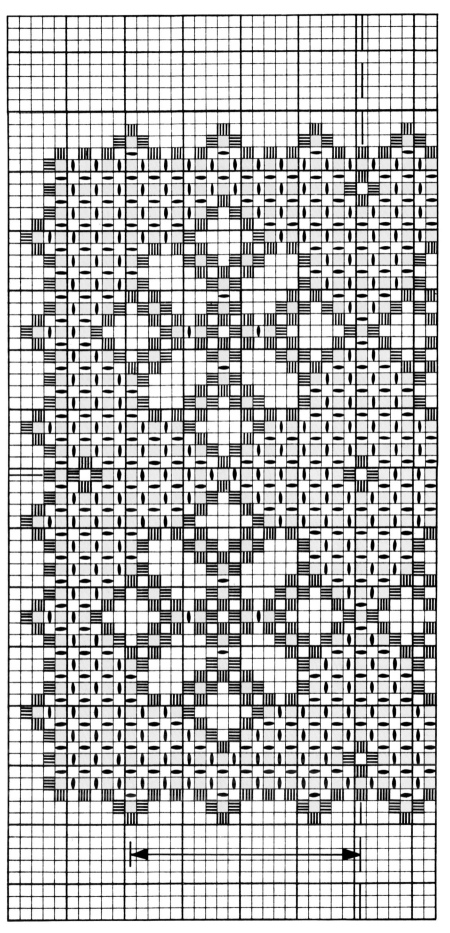

Chart for pages 68, 69 and 71.

Cushion covers with cross-stitch roses ✥ ✥ ✥ ✥ ✥ ✥

BELLANA 3256
> *Satin-stitch motifs*: Pearl No. 5
> *Overcasting*: Pearl No. 8
> *Cross-stitch motifs*: Three strands of embroidery twist
> *Back stitch*: One strand of embroidery twist

You can either embroider the roses first and then work the Hardanger border around them, as big as you like, or work the border and then put the roses in afterwards. Mark the central lines with tacking anyway, so you do not get disorientated.

Cross-stitch instructions

First of all, work the cross-stitch motifs, then outline the flowers with back stitch and embroider the tiny details on top of the cross stitch. The dark outlines mean that even pale colours stand out well against the background and they can be used on any colour of fabric.

On the cross-stitch chart, 1 square = 2 threads
On the Hardanger chart, 1 square = 4 threads

> *You will find the charts on pages 78, 80 and 81.*

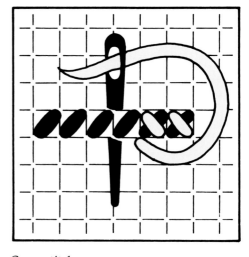

Cross-stitch.

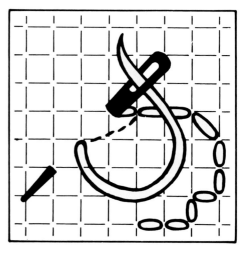

Back stitch.

For cushions A and B the reference points for laying out the roses are marked on the Hardanger chart on page 78.

A. Bellana 3256/264

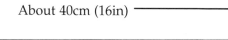

About 40cm (16in)

B. Bellana 3256/618

Position the flower motif on the fabric, working outwards from the centre of the cushion.

C. BELLANA 3256/430

About 40cm (16in)

Put one rose in the corner and scatter the leaves about wherever you like.

D. BELLANA 3256/101

Chart for pages 74 and 75.

1

- ∵ light rush green
- N mint green
- ● ivy green
- ꝰ dark old rose
- T medium old rose
- V light old rose
- ꞇ pearl rose
- · white

2

- ╱ lime green
- ✗ olive
- ↓ silver fir
- ▲ coral red
- Y flamingo
- ✚ light gold
- ❘ cream

3

- ✗ olive green
- ◢ laurel green
- ∵ light rush green
- ꟊ fuchsia
- ⳑ pale pink
- — soft pink
- · white

4

- ✗ olive green
- ◢ laurel green
- ∵ light rush green
- ꝰ dark old rose
- K crimson
- ~ reddish orange

5

- ✗ olive green
- ∵ light rush green
- H pink
- o medium pink
- — soft pink
- · white
- ✚ light gold

6

- ✗ olive green
- ⌐ light green
- o medium pink
- — soft pink

꜏ Outline for all roses: dark grey.

7

- ✗ olive green
- ⌐ light green
- ■ yellow ochre
- Z sunshine yellow
- ✚ light gold
- ❘ cream
- · white

8

- ➐ moss green
- ✗ olive green
- ■ yellow ochre
- ~ reddish orange
- ◀ yellowish orange

9

- ◢ laurel green
- ✗ olive green
- ⌐ light green
- ◢ dark gold
- S pale yellow
- ❘ cream
- · white

Key for colours on cross-stitch charts on pages 80 and 81.

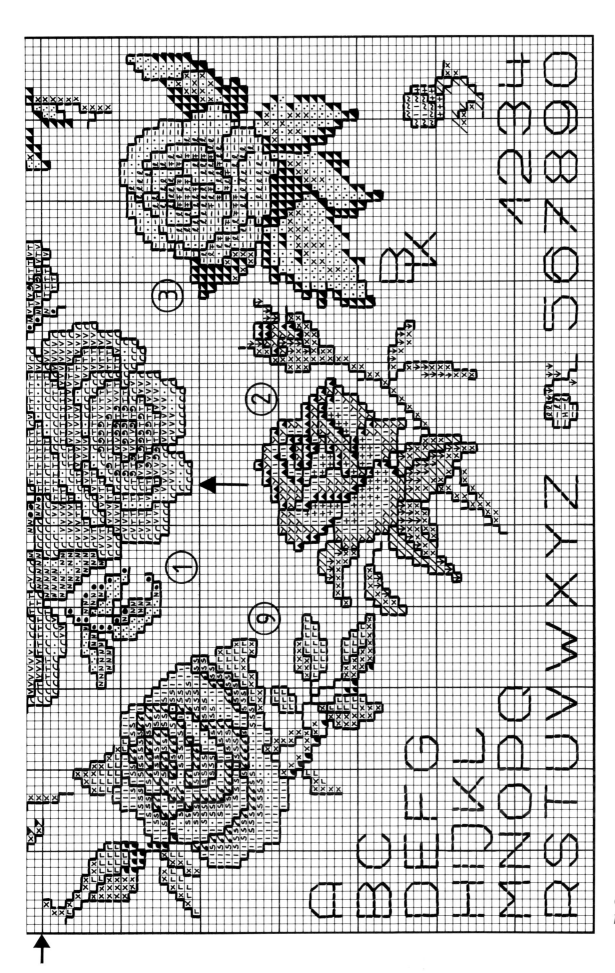

*Chart for
pages 74–77.*

Christmas tablemats

EMBROIDERY THREAD

Satin-stitch motifs: Pearl No. 3
Scalloped border: Pearl No. 5
Securing the edge: two strands of embroidery twist, plus sewing thread
Overcasting: Pearl No. 5 and gold thread
Dove's-eye filling stitch: Pearl No. 5
Star stitch: Pearl No. 5 and gold thread

For details of how to make the scalloped edge, see page 84.

Undercloth (A)

ARIOSA 3711/687

Size of embroidery: 668 x 668 threads
Ariosa: about 90 x 90cm (35 x 35in)
Davosa: about 95 x 95cm (37 x 37in)
Size of fabric: about 105 x 105cm (41 x 41in)

Key

 Scalloped border: dark green

Poinsettia (C)

DAVOSA 3770/954

Size of embroidery: 388 x 396 threads
Davosa: about 55 x 55cm (22 x 22in)
Ariosa: about 52 x 52cm (20½ x 20½in)
Size of fabric: about 65 x 65cm (25½ x 25½in)

Key

|||| *Satin stitch*: dark red
 Satin stitch: green
 Overcasting: green
 Overcasting: gold
☐ *Cut out*
 Scalloped border: dark red

You will find the charts on pages 86 and 87.

Christmas rose (B)

ARIOSA 3711/100

Size of embroidery: 340 x 340 threads
Ariosa: about 45 x 45cm (18 x 18in)
Davosa: about 48 x 48cm (19 x 19in)
Size of fabric: about 55 x 55cm (22 x 22in)

You will find the chart on page 86.

Scalloped border

The strengthened edge is carried out in three stages.

1. Work satin stitches with two strands of embroidery twist the same colour as the background fabric, following the Hardanger chart.

2. Sew a line with a sewing machine set for 1mm stitches (25 stitches to the inch) .

3. Now work the scalloped border, using Pearl No. 5 on top of the embroidery-twist stitches. At each corner, work five stitches into the same point of entry.

4. Finally, cut off the fabric close to the scalloped border.

Key

▥	*Satin stitch*: white
⬮	*Overcasting*: gold
⬯	*Overcasting*: white
⬮	*Overcasting*: light green
◇	*Dove's-eye filling stitch*: light green
▢	*Cut out*
▦	*Scalloped border*: white
▩	*Star stitch*: gold
✳	*Star stitch*: pink

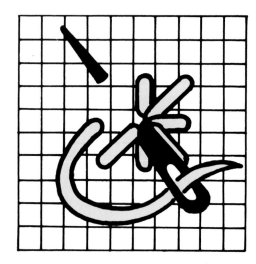

Star stitch.

Scalloped border.

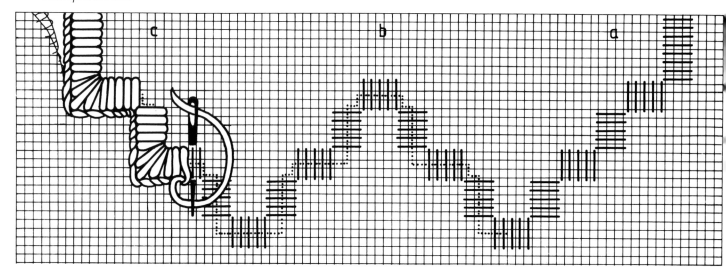

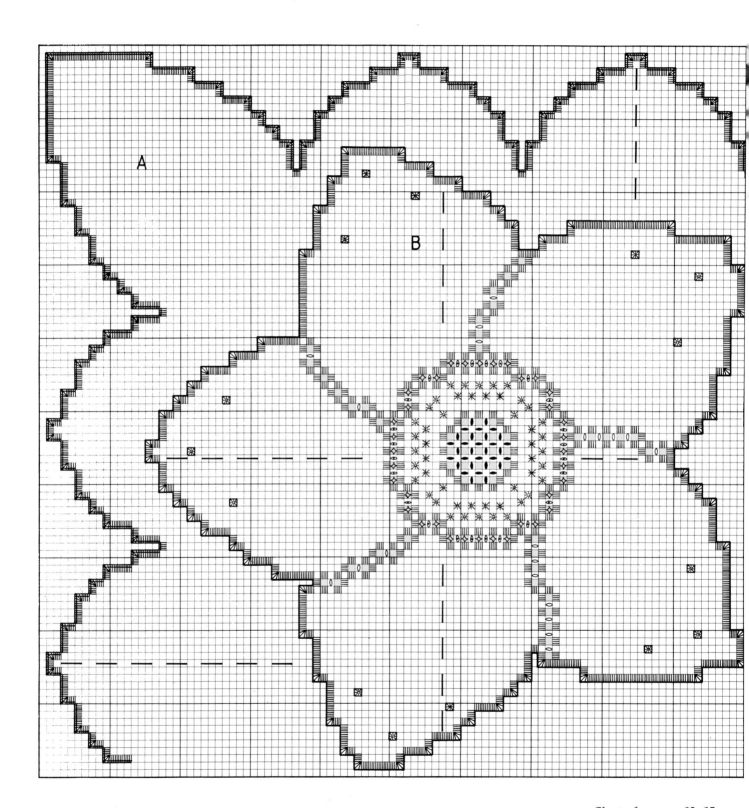

Charts for pages 82–85.

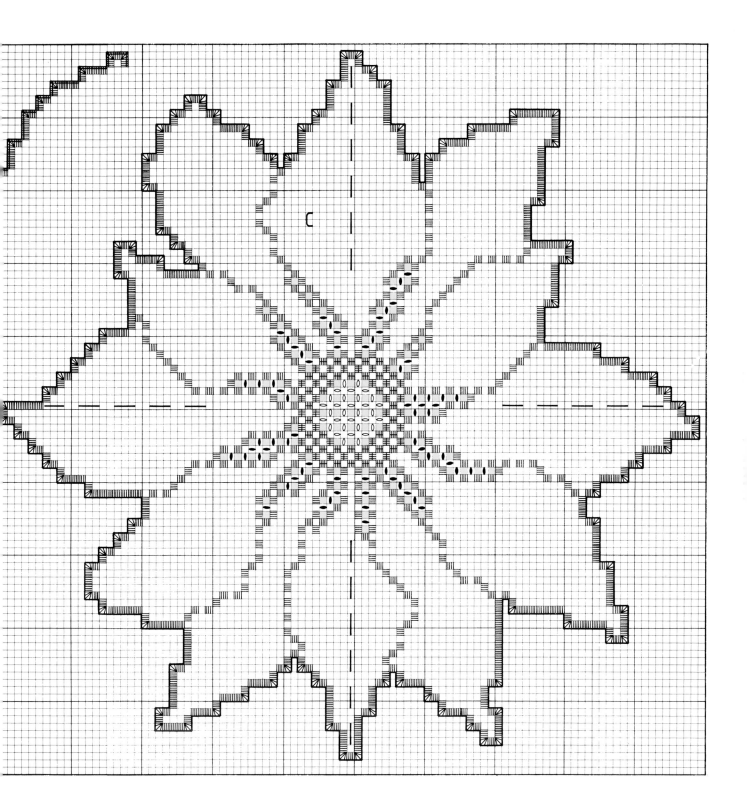

C

Caring for your work

Openwork and lacy embroideries should be handled carefully, so here are some tips on caring for them:

If you do not want to wash your work by hand (which is without doubt the kindest thing to do), you should always put it in a laundry net or pillowcase to protect it from unnecessary stresses and strains in the washing process. You should never spin dry or tumble dry any sort of openwork, because the structure of the fabric gets loosened in all that pulling and tumbling around.

Iron your work on the wrong side, using a damp cloth.

Washing and ironing temperatures should be those of the 'weakest link': in other words, if you have used gold or silver thread, your washing temperature should not exceed 30°C (86°F) and you should iron on a low setting, even if the material can be washed at 95°C (203°F) and ironed with a hot iron. Basically, you just need to follow the care instructions given by the embroidery-thread manufacturer.

To keep the colours unchanged, always use washing powder without optical brighteners.

Following these simple rules will keep your precious work in good condition and will retain its charm for years to come.

Index